Field Trips

At the Farm

By Sophie Geister-Jones

level 2
little blue readers

www.littlebluehousebooks.com

Little Blue House is distributed by North Star Editions:
sales@northstareditions.com | 888-417-0195

Produced for Little Blue House by Red Line Editorial.

Photographs ©: Image Source/iStockphoto, cover; Maksymowicz/iStockphoto, 4, 24 (bottom right); Iakov Filimonov/Shutterstock Images, 6–7; AlinaMD/iStockphoto, 9 (top); Drazen_/iStockphoto, 9 (bottom), 24 (top right); wwing/iStockphoto, 11; ClarkandCompany/iStockphoto, 12; branex/iStockphoto, 14–15; Tanes Ngamsom/iStockphoto, 17; republica/iStockphoto, 18–19; martinedoucet/iStockphoto, 20 (top); boggy22/iStockphoto, 20 (bottom); skynesher/iStockphoto, 22–23; georgeclerk/iStockphoto, 24 (top left); mtreasure/iStockphoto, 24 (bottom left)

Library of Congress Control Number: 2019908667

ISBN
978-1-64619-028-7 (hardcover)
978-1-64619-067-6 (paperback)
978-1-64619-106-2 (ebook pdf)
978-1-64619-145-1 (hosted ebook)

Printed in the United States of America
Mankato, MN
012020

About the Author

Sophie Geister-Jones likes reading, spending time with her family, and eating cheese. She lives in Minnesota.

Table of Contents

At the Farm

We go on a field trip to the farm.

We see a tractor in a field.

The tractor can pull

heavy things.

We meet the farmers.

They show us some

baby cows.

Next we see a field full
of corn.

We also see a field with
many sunflowers.

We see a big red barn in one of the fields.
The farmer says we can go inside.

Barn Animals

Many animals live inside the barn.

We see a cat sitting on a pole.

The cat lives in the barn.

We walk through the barn and see cows.
The farmers get milk from these cows.

The farmers also keep goats inside the barn. The goats have little horns on their heads.

Pigs live in the barn too.

They play in the mud.

Outside the Barn

Next we go outside

the barn.

We help feed the chickens.

We see a dog on the farm.

We pet the dog.

We like being on the farm.

Glossary

chicken

sunflower

cow

tractor

Index